GOLDEN RETRIEVER

Training & Breed Overview

THE WOOF BROTHERS

Contents

Preface

Hi, we are The Woof Brothers.

We are a group started by siblings, and our purpose is to help you in all aspects of raising, training, and enjoying the company of your four legged best friend(s).

You may have grabbed this book because you just adopted or bought a new doggy bundle of joy.

Perhaps you are looking for some help with house training your new canine roommate.

Maybe you have an energy filled teenager who jumps, chews, and leash pulls...

... Or you simply want to get more information on how you can better communicate with your guy or gal. (everyone has seen their dog's face turn sideways in confusion as they say a command)

Whatever the reason, **we thank you for reading and checking this book out.**

This book is dedicated entirely to teaching you what our group has learned, and helping you have the best relationship possible with your dog. No fluff, just real techniques, that really work.

Our Story

There is something about dogs' unconditional love and loyalty that makes people crazy about them. That is how it all started for all of us at The Woof Brothers.

Dogs have saved our lives and taught us more about ourselves than any of the training we raised on to them.

The Woof Brothers consists of not only trainers, but overall dog lovers, and pet owners, who combined all their knowledge to help pass it on to others.

We hope our work helps dog owners achieve a better understanding of their four legged friends and helps lessen the abandonment of dogs, which sadly happens more and more. We believe that if we all took some of the lessons dogs teach us the world would be a better place.

So let's be more like our dog today and live in the moment, not be spiteful, hold no grudges, and see no ethnicity or race.

To find out more and stay updated on our future releases follow us on our social medias -

Instagram & Facebook: @the.woof.brothers

Youtube: The Woof Brothers

ONE

Introduction & History of the Breed

G olden Retrievers are one of the most popular dog breeds in the world. This is with good reason. Goldens are loyal, dependable dogs that make great additions to most families. Often, they are used as service dogs because they are so eager to please. They are nurturing in nature and form great partnerships with their human companions. It is undeniably a breed that embodies the saying "mans best friend".

Golden Retrievers have quite the history assisting and partnering with humans despite their brief existence. The breed is only slightly over 140 years old. That is how young the breed is! There are breeds like the 'chow chow' where there is evidence of them being domesticated back in 206 BC. So it may come as a surprise, but Golden Retrievers are still a young breed in the vast lineage of dog breeds we have today.

Their origin begins in Scotland where older generations of retrievers were assistants to hunters. Retrievers would accompany hunters and 'retrieve' shot game undamaged.

While hunting in marshy areas however, the Scottish hunters would encounter problems. Their Retrievers would be hesitant to access those areas as they were not very willing to get wet. The hunters needed to come up with a solution to have a perfect hunting dog. The answer came when they bred their Retrievers with Water Spaniels. This mix created the loveable dog breed known today as the Golden Retriever. Breeding programs for Golden Retrievers have been in place since the 19th century, and they continue to flourish today as they are amongst the most sought after canines in the world.

Today we find Golden Retrievers in an array of different golden shades (dark gold, light gold, cream, white, and even a reddish gold). The reason Golden Retrievers have these shades is thanks to a breeder named Dudley Marjoribanks. He adopted a retriever with a yellowish coat, despite being born amongst a litter with black coats. Dudley bred his yellow-coated retriever with a water spaniel. This is what truly developed the 'Golden' Retriever. The intelligent golden hunting dog quickly rose in popularity from the mid-1860s, and the American Kennel Club (AKC) officially recognized Golden Retrievers in 1925.

There are three types of Golden Retriever - English, American and Canadian. There are subtle differences between the types of Goldens, but they all fall under the same breed.

Fact Source: Embracepetinsurance.com. (2019). *6 Fun Facts You Probably Didn't Know about Golden Retrievers*. [online] Available at: https://www.embracepetinsurance. com/waterbowl/article/6-fun-facts-about-golden-retrievers

A purebred Golden Retriever is considered a medium to large size dog. Females grow up to an average of 22 inches in height and weigh around 60 pounds. Males grow up to 24 inches in height and weigh around 70 pounds. They have litters of around 8 puppies and live between 10-13 years.

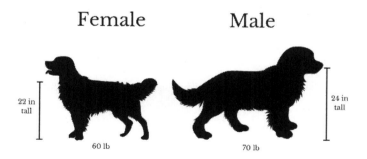

Female   Male

22 in tall   24 in tall

60 lb   70 lb

This breed hasn't been around long, but it has definitely

made an impression. They are intelligent, eager to learn, loyal and lovable companions. Goldens have a soft spot in our hearts, and we definitely recommend adopting one of these fur-balls.

Behavior

Adopting a Golden Retriever (or any dog) is an awesome feeling. You may have heard or done some research and found out that Goldens are very intelligent and social dogs. They are energetic dogs with a trustworthy, confident, and friendly temperament. While these things are all great and true, Goldens do need to be in an environment where they can thrive. They are an active breed, so they require a minimum of an hour of exercise a day. They have a good appetite, so without this daily workout they will gain weight fast. If they aren't in an optimal environment, even the smartest and calmest of Golden Retrievers will act up.

It is important for prospective owners to be honest with themselves and question if they are able and willing to take care of a Golden. They should ask themselves... do they have the time, space, and support needed to adopt? If you are thinking about adopting a Golden, and you can provide the correct environment, he or she will undoubtedly reward you with loyalty and loving companionship. As we mentioned above the breed has a history of partnering with people. This partnership will be clear from an early age. A puppy will constantly want to be with you and even show signs of mimicking your behavior. This playful attitude remains for most of its life as it is a breed that is always willing to play, swim, run, and cuddle next to you.

In the right environment Goldens are kind in nature, and bond strongly with their families. They are social dogs that get along well with other animals, children, and even strangers. This book summarizes this special breed, and helps guide you in different areas including grooming, communication, and training. We encourage all Golden owners/moms/dads, new and seasoned to read though it in its entirety. There will be useful tips and facts you may not have considered or known about your four-legged friend.

Family Dynamic

Some breeds are naturally independent and distant. Golden Retrievers definitely do not fall in this category. All dogs are individuals and display their own unique characteristics but in general, Goldens shower the whole family with affection. They cannot stand loneliness and always love having a play companion. This is why they adapt well to apartment/home living. As long as they get enough exercise they are happy even in the smallest of apartments. Overall, they are the ideal family dog for all ages.

Introducing a new pet to young children can be challenging. Kids usually mean well but there is a thin line between petting and hitting at a young age. Also, those tight cuddly hugs can come awfully close to a chokehold. Sometimes, children need time and guidance with how to handle animals. Certain breeds and pets can make this a difficult task to learn. They react unpredictably to children's natural behaviors. Golden Retrievers form the perfect counterbalance. Since their personalities are so laid back, they are the perfect dog for a child to learn about respecting animals from. They are patient and sturdy enough to handle the chaos a child can create. A Golden will allow a child to make mistakes and learn how to handle them without parents having to fear of a nip or an accident occurring.

Kids never seem to run out of energy and neither do Goldens!

We believe that it is very beneficial to introduce children to dogs at a young age. Especially Goldens are a great choice. As we had mentioned before Goldens are a very relaxed, friendly, and adaptable breed. Add this to the fact that they are easily trained and you have a great family pet for children of all ages. They are a loyal breed, and as a result, they will bond to the family and the members within their family. This means they will feel responsible for your children.

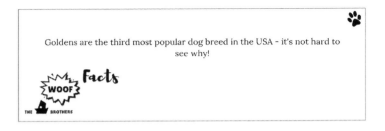

Goldens are the third most popular dog breed in the USA - it's not hard to see why!

Fact Source: American Kennel Club. (2019). *Golden Retriever Dog Breed Information*. [online] Available at: https://www.akc.org/dog-breeds/golden-retriever/.

Adopting a Golden is also a great gateway to teaching children about responsibility. A family takes care of one another. In order for a Golden to take care of your family, it needs the family to take care of it. Children can grasp this concept well and will find fun in handling their responsibilities as pet owners. Feeding, training, and walking are all things that benefit both parties greatly.

Golden Retrievers are some of the best companion animals. Once they form a bond with your child, it will be a lifelong partnership. They will seek to protect your child and also find joy in the companionship. You will always have someone to look out for your children and teach them how to be responsible.

How Do They Get Along With Other Pets?

Friendliness towards humans and friendliness towards other animals are two completely different things. As we mentioned above Goldens were bred to be hunters assistants. Many believe this means they have an instinctual desire to chase and hunt down other animals. This is simply not true. Goldens generally won't chase, but things in flight can distract them and catch their eyes. A ball or bird in flight will naturally get their attention, and can cause them to go after it.

Goldens will snuggle and get along with just about everyone. Owners have even successfully had their Golden be best friends with parrots and hamsters!

Fact Source: Keady, C. (2019). *HuffPost is now a part of Oath*. Huffpost.com. Available at: https://www.huffpost.com/entry/golden-retriever-hamster-birds-friends_n_7738510.

Other Dogs

There are many factors that come into play that determine how Goldens will get along with other pets in a home. The breeds laid back and playful attitude is usually accommodating to most other dogs. A big determining factor for dogs getting along is their environment when born. When a puppy is born its first 6 to 8 weeks of life are incredibly crucial to its development. Its mother and littermates help it learn good canine social skills which affect how it treats other dogs for the rest of its life. If a young Golden or any dog could not learn these vital social skills early on it will misbehave when meeting other dogs or pets. Most breeds will coexist peacefully and happily if they were able to develop with their mother and littermates. It helps to research the personality and temperament of the dog you want to mix with your Golden to make sure they can get along. In certain cases it is helpful to consult a veterinarian. Introducing a new dog into your home can be stressful and you want to make sure that your Golden and any other dogs are happy.

A Cats Best Friend?

Goldens are a breed that can get along well with their feline counterparts. You may have already noticed a trend, but Golden Retrievers generally love everyone. The loyal, enthusiastic, and intelligent breed is very accepting of cats and there are many instances of them forming close bonds. We suggest however, that the first encounter should be supervised and managed. Every dog is an individual and a mix of its genetics, training, and environment. Please realize this and introduce new animals to one another safely. Family or packs are important to Goldens. Once it understands that another animal is part of the family unit, there should be little problem with the two interacting.

In summary; Golden Retrievers have great personalities and this extends to their interactions with other animals. You will have more luck and success introducing your Golden to other animals than most other breeds. This can take a lot of stress off of you when you want all of your fur babies to get along.

If there are no Goldens in heaven... I'm not going!

TWO

Purchasing a Golden

In this section of the book, we will have a look at what prospective owners should consider when adopting a Golden Retriever. There are several things to think about when bringing a Golden home. Adopting a Golden is truly life changing. Do not rush the process and get enough information to make sure you're prepared.

We will consider all the following options and differences:

- Differences between a male and a female?
- A puppy or an older Golden?
- Care costs.
- Breeder and adoption choices.

We cannot stress it enough but adopting one of these adorable fur-balls is a big commitment. If you are not adopting by yourself, talk as a family about the responsibilities each person will have.

Making Sure You Are Prepared

While introducing this breed we went over the many bene-fits and positives that are associated with Goldens. They are friendly and known for their devoted and obedient nature as family companions. These traits make them very popular. We want to make sure however, that potential adopters are prepared for the responsibilities that come with taking care of the breed. They need a minimum of one hour of exercise every day. Ignoring a Goldens active nature will eventually lead to behavior problems, poor health, and an unhappy dog. They need a task or job to release their energy. A happy and healthy Golden is calm at home, and enthusiastic when out playing.

Plenty of exercise is not the only thing one needs to prepare for. They also have a dense long water repellent coat that needs frequent care. Goldens coats need brushing at least twice a week. They are a breed that sheds... a lot. If you are a neat freak, you may need to do some extra meditating while sharing your home with a Golden.

Lastly, Goldens are very social. This makes them excellent family dogs but also makes them especially dependent. They can act up when alone for long periods of time without a playing partner. If you and your family are away from home often, it will definitely break your Goldens heart.

Golden Retrievers can suffer from separation anxiety. They are such social animals that they can struggle when kept apart from their owners.

Fact Source: The Happy Puppy Site. (2019). *Golden Retriever Facts - 40 Amazing Things You Never Knew - The Happy Puppy Site*. Available at: https://thehappypuppysite.com/golden-retriever-facts/.

Male or Female?

There are physical and behavioral differences between a male and a female Golden Retriever. A male will weigh around sixty-five pounds while females generally weigh fifty-five pounds. Females are also known to be a little shorter than males. Males have slightly longer coats and carry more muscle mass than a female. The other difference in their structure is their head and nose. A male's head and nose will be broader than a females.

If you are trying to decide the best fit for your family, keep in mind that it is common for a male Golden to latch onto who they perceive as the alpha male. This means that males become more fixated and loyal to one owner. This is great if your Golden is only your companion, but in a family dynamic a female may be more suitable. Both males and females react to the mood and vibe their owners give off. So they will both show loyalty and companionship to their owners, just generally females will not share the same devotion to one "alpha" leader like a male would.

A female Golden Retriever will often be more headstrong and independent in character than a male Golden. This is their main difference in temperament. Please remember though, that both males and females will be loyal to their family and gentle with any kids. The slight differences they have in temperament does not mean they will not bond with their family or owners. To a Golden Retriever, you as their pack and family is the most important thing. They will form bonds and attachments to each member of their family/pack. It might just be that a male or female fits your family dynamic better.

Puppy or Adult?

Puppies are adorable... but they are also little energetic balls of chaos. Adult Goldens are also adorable... but were they trained properly and will you have the same bond as you would with a puppy you raised? The decision to get a puppy or an adult Golden is a personal one. It depends on several things such as your time, budget, and needs. Both options offer their own set of unique benefits and challenges.

Adopting Puppies

Puppies are babies that are still developing. It is cute to see them exploring the world and learning something new with every clumsy step. However, being "babies" means they need time, attention, and loads of training. For the entire first year of your puppy's life, you are teaching it the basic skills it needs to go through life, and this can be time consuming. They also have tons of energy and if they do not get enough exercise (when is enough ever enough for a puppy?) then it might even seem like they are bouncing off the walls. They will take plenty of naps, but this means they are charging up and will be ready for more games and stimulation afterwards.

Besides this time commitment, there are also some extra costs involved with raising a puppy. There is not only the adoption fee but also added costs of vaccinations, spaying and neutering, training and socialization classes. New equipment like leashes, bows, toys, and more will also need to be purchased. They will grow incredibly fast, so expect a new pup to outgrow certain toys and gear quickly.

Puppies are a great addition to the family, but you need consider if you can put in the time to train your puppy the way you want them to behave. What they learn in their formative years will be their foundation as they grow up.

Adopting Adults

An older dog will usually have completed some training and will be up to date on vaccines. They will bring all their good habits... and all their bad habits. You have probably heard the saying, "You cannot teach an old dog new tricks." Well, this is not true, but it is very difficult and frustrating trying to break an older dog's bad habits. It will take more time to correct a habit in an older dog than to teach a puppy. Shelters and rescue groups will often train their dogs to be social and well behaved. This increases their chances of being adopted and decreases their chance of being brought back or abandoned.

Adult Goldens don't need the constant looking after a puppy needs but there is still a large time commitment required. The exercise needs do not disappear and they also require more mental stimulation. If you and your family are gone for most of the day or travel a lot and are not able to bring your Golden, we recommend hiring a dog walker or sitter.

Seniors

For those who cannot be as active but are looking to adopt a Golden there are options available. It is possible to adopt a senior Golden Retriever. They are more relaxed and their exercise needs are not as extreme as puppies or adults. Health issues are more prevalent and you must be prepared for end-of-life care. Senior Goldens can be a great option for some as they are great cuddle buddies and have a more meager energy level.

Whether you get a puppy, adult or senior Golden it will be a rewarding experience. It is all about making an informed decision and adopting the match that fits your lifestyle.

Care Costs and Breeder Choices

Now you have an accurate picture of a Golden Retriever's demeanor, their personality, and which age best suits your lifestyle. In the following section, we will delve into the costs that come with adopting a Golden Retriever. Remember, these costs will fluctuate and vary, and we are providing estimates. Depending on your situation and location it could be lower or higher than what you see reflected here.

Health

Goldens light up any room they walk into with their positive energy, but unfortunately they risk suffering from some extreme health issues. This is especially true when they come from a disreputable breeder. With the rise in the breeds popularity came a rise of ill-intentioned breeders. These breeders only see dollar signs and are not concerned with good breeding practices. Unfortunately, this increases health risks for Goldens. A breeder that ensures good lineage for their puppies will produce healthier dogs. Far fewer health complications will come up if there is a clear health history of the parents available. We will discuss more health concerns in the "health" section of this book. Overall, we recommend to always ask for a Goldens parenting and health history.

You might have heard of and considered pet insurance. It is a great idea if you get your Golden as a puppy. Pet insurers are very strict about pre-existing conditions. So, it is great and helpful if you have covered your puppy who has no known history of illness. It is less effective to get pet insurance on an older Golden who might have had illnesses in the past. Pet insurance and human insurance operate differently. While pet insurance helps with the cost of unexpected vet bills, owners have to file the claim themselves and wait to be reimbursed. A vet will not file for you.

The lower baseline for purchasing a Golden will be $500. This will probably be from a home breeder, or a pet store. They often include vaccinations in their price, but if it does not include this, you can expect to pay $20-$150. Health insurance varies by state and zip code but is generally around $40 per month.

On average, owning a Golden can cost you $15,000 over his lifetime.

Fact Source: Guthrie, M. (2019). *Golden Retriever Cost - How Much Does A Golden Cost To Buy And Raise.* [online] The Happy Puppy Site. Available at: https://thehappypuppysite.com/golden-retriever-price/.

Breeders

Having proof of a Goldens health history and the history of its parents requires documentation. The American Kennel Club (AKC) is the leading authority on all things dogs. AKC documentation shows that your dog is a pure breed and comes from healthy parents. It also ensures that the breeders you are buying from are legitimate.

AKC documentation is especially crucial if you want a dog you can show or place in events. Without the proper registration, they cannot take part in any AKC events. The AKC has the largest registry that proves a dogs bloodline. There are breeders who claim to have AKC registration and then turn out not to have it. If the registration is important to you, make sure the breeder hands you the registration application. If they do not, don't let them coerce you into buying the dog.

Meeting a breeder can be an overwhelming experience. It helps to know what to expect before you go into a meeting with them. A good breeder will not waste their time trying to scam you or miss small details so there is nothing to fear. One of the first things to look out for is a contract. A good breeder will have a contract that will protect you, the puppy, and themselves if anything goes wrong during the adoption process. You want to make sure that the breeder can present you with a certificate of health. All proper breeders will have established documentation that proves their puppies are healthy and have received the care appropriate for their age.

You may have a long list of questions to ask your breeder, and that is perfect! They should be happy at your interest and care level before adopting. We have made a short list of questions you should ask your breeder and you can add to:

- Has the puppy been examined for common health problems like hip dysplasia?
- Do you have certificates of health for the puppies?
- Do you have a contract for each puppy?
- Do you have a vet assess your puppies before you let a buyer take them home?
- How are the puppies socialized?

Be prepared for a breeder to ask you questions in return. A good breeder will want to know that their puppy is going to a good home, and so they will ask about the environment you will keep the puppy in. Both parties should be upfront and honest with their answers and expectations and it will make the whole process a breeze.

Goldens with AKC registration and excellent bloodlines will cost around $1500. These dogs may cost more upfront but it can mean far fewer costs in terms of vet bills.

Shelters

Sometimes you can get lucky and find shelters/rescues that hold adoption events with Golden Retrievers. Their focus is on placing a dog in a great home. There are more unknowns in terms of health but you will still get a great family dog. At these shelters or rescue centers it is possible to adopt from $200-$400.

All you need is love... and a Golden Retriever!

THREE

Welcoming Your New Best Friend Home

INTRODUCING YOUR GOLDEN TO A NEW ENVIRONMENT

Whether you are bringing a puppy or an adult Golden home dog there is some prep involved. Dog proofing your home is an underrated but essential task. If you don't want some of your favorite possessions destroyed in the first few months of your new roommate moving in, then don't take this step lightly. Dog proofing not only benefits your belongings, it also keeps your new dog safe. It is impossible to keep your eyes on your new dog 24/7 and it will amaze you how fast they can get themselves into trouble.

Take this opportunity to do anything that will help facilitate the relationship you hope to create with your dog. We have outlined the main things to keep in mind when dog proofing your home.

At what age should a puppy come home?

There is a lot of conflicting information out regarding when you should first bring a puppy home. One of the most important things you want to keep in mind is that you want to avoid traumatizing your new puppy. The transition to a new environment is overwhelming for a puppy that is too young, and can lead to behavioral issues as it grows up. Research has shown that Goldens removed from their littermates too early in life develop issues like anxiety, over-possessiveness, aggression, and even have difficulties in learning and training.

Why would these issues come up?

Puppies learn important lessons from their mother and littermates. These lessons are not something that humans can replicate and replace for young Goldens. Puppies learn a lot more than you would first imagine from their mother.

One of these important lessons is to gain the ability to understand instructions and accept being disciplined. A mother will quickly discipline a young puppy who gets out of line. This creates a very important foundation of learning for the puppy. They learn that pushing the boundaries leads to consequences. As a result, you will have an easier time training them if they stayed with their mother for the appropriate amount of time. Further benefits of leaving a puppy with its mom and litter include them not biting, learning how to get touched and cuddled often, and an ability to decipher who the leader of the pack is and who to follow. All these learned behaviors help create a Goldens lovable personality. As adorable as puppies may be, we are doing them a disservice by taking them away from their litters too soon.

We feel that the ideal age to bring a puppy home is at eight weeks old. By taking your puppy home at eight weeks, you allow it to get all the nurturing and foundations it needs to live a long and socially balanced life. The little gal or guy will definitely still be young enough to be open to new experiences and bond with you. This is the perfect medium.

What should I have at home?

There are a host of things you will want to get when you are bringing a puppy or dog home for the first time. Here is a list of the things you cannot skip out on having:

- Food & treats
- Food & water bowls
- Collar
- Tag for ID
- Bed for the dog to sleep in
- A crate
- Leash/Harness*

---

*There is much debate about whether owners should use a harness or a leash. The reason people avoid leashes is that they can lead to a dog inadvertently choking themselves. Plus, harnesses give more support to you as the owner when walking the dog. Leashes are also perfectly fine for controlling a dog. We feel that it comes down to personal preference, and the relationship between you and your dog.

Getting your dog an ID tag is essential for if he or she gets lost. Your contact information will be on there and a kind-hearted person will assist getting your dog back to you. Some owners also microchip their dogs. This requires quite some extra steps and a veterinarians scan. An ID tag is far more essential. A person can quickly and easily see that the dog has a home and contact the owner.

Having a Golden also means an owner will need to adapt to a fur cleaning regiment. Goldens coats have a light odor and they shed... a lot. To combat this and keep your home clean you should consider adding the following items to your shopping list:

- Shampoo
- A brush (furminator is a good brand)
- Doggy poop bags
- Toothpaste and toothbrush*

---

*Dental health is just as important as making sure their coat stays tangle free. There are many special brands of toothpaste made just for dogs. The sooner you get in the routine of teeth brushing, the easier it will be for you and your Golden. If you are unsure of what products to use, consult your vet. They should have some available or sell them in their office. Owners can work up to brushing daily, but three days a week can already make a difference for a healthy mouth.

Toys are also very important for the development of your Golden. They help keep those little curious minds stimulated! Toys serve multiple functions. They are a great way for you to bond, and they also keep your new four legged bestie occupied and away from destroying your furniture. A bored dog is a naughty dog, so do not give them an opportunity to cause mischief. Get lots of stimulating toys to ensure that your Golden is occupied and happy.

The first image ever uploaded to Instagram was a picture of a Golden Retriever in 2010!

Fact Source: The Happy Puppy Site. (2019). *Golden Retriever Facts - 40 Amazing Things You Never Knew - The Happy Puppy Site*. [online] Available at: https://thehappypuppysite.com/golden-retriever-facts/.

Dog Proofing

Dog proofing your home is not something many people are familiar with. All too often people think they can just bring a dog home with little to no preparation. This couldn't be farther from the truth. New owners need to make sure that their home is ready to receive a new four-legged family member. This starts by making sure the house is safe for the new gal or guy, and that your favorite items are out of their reach.

Chewers and sniffers! Dogs, but especially Goldens explore with their nose and mouth. They will follow any interesting scent and then lick or chew on it. All tiny toys and other small items can be choking hazards and will have to be put away. Cleaning products and medicines need to be locked away or up high where your Golden will not get to. Wires in your home can also present issues. If there are any protruding wires, cover them up with some electrical tape and try to hide them from view. If there is a room that has too many wires to protect, make it off-limits to your Golden. Section it off so they cannot get in there.

Trash cans are usually filled with all kinds of interesting scents... at least your Golden thinks so! Make sure your garbage can is sturdy and up to the job of protecting trash from your Golden. Goldens are inquisitive and if they can get their snout in it, then you can bet they will chew on it. You do not want to walk into a room that is showered with garbage or a sick Golden who ate the wrong thing. Save yourself and everyone the heartache by getting a sturdy trash can.

Driving a Golden Home

Bringing home a new dog is very exciting! It can also be a stressful experience for your dog. We recommend getting help from a family member or friend with transporting the dog home. This way one person can focus on driving and the other can calm the dog down if this becomes necessary.

Before the trip it would be best for your Golden to have gone to the bathroom. We also recommend bringing a towel and laying it over your backseat. This will give you some protection in case your Golden has an accident or vomits. Sometimes nausea occurs on car rides, they can get motion sickness just like the best of us. It is best to have the dog in a car harness on the back seat but traveling in a crate is also fine.

Once they are home, you can begin establishing some rules and a schedule for your Golden.

Training & Socialization Introduction

Winging it is never the best technique, and a Golden loves structure. Socialization is a great first thing to introduce to a new dog. Socialization is the process of getting a dog comfortable with its surroundings. You want your new family member to get used to you, your home, and the family members or other pets inside your home. This is just the beginning, as they also need to be socialized with everything outside of your home. A Golden should get to know the neighborhood, other dogs, and people around them.

Training is essential to having a happy and well balanced Golden. We will get deeper into training later on, but we want to stress the importance of starting early with training. Although this book will help you with training at home, we still recommend joining a training program. Not only will your Golden learn new tricks and behave better, he or she will also interact with other dogs. Humans and dogs are social animals, having these interactions will benefit all parties.

Crate Training

When dogs want to relax or rest they instinctually look for a den. So if you notice your dog laying under things like your coffee table or curtains it is natural behavior. Therefore, crate training is an important process and one that most Goldens respond favorably to. Especially when a Golden is younger, crate training is very beneficial. A crate is simply a safe "den" for when they aren't being supervised. It is completely up to you the owner to decide if your Goldens crate is also where they sleep or if they also have a bed. As we mentioned above, a crate is meant to be a safe controlled space for your dog to relax in. It is not a place for "time-outs" or a place for punishment. It is a positive and happy place. Goldens are social dogs, and you and your Golden will benefit if you keep the crate in an area of the house where your dog can see and interact with you or your family.

Purchasing a crate can be nerve-wrecking. Keep in mind that if you still have a young Golden, they grow quickly. You will want to buy a crate large enough for them to lie in, stand in, sit in, and move around in. There are adaptable crate options available. These allow you to adjust the size of the crate to the size of your dog. They can definitely become lifesavers for these quickly growing gals and guys.

The crate needs to have a comfortable blanket and some toys in it. Do not expect your dog to just go lay in an empty box with no comfort and nothing to do. A Golden loves positive reinforcement; you will have more luck using those methods than negative ones.

We have some tips for getting your Golden comfortable with their crate. Try to avoid placing him or her in the crate when they are in a high energy state. Take them for a walk or play with them before introducing the crate to them. A tired Golden will be more receptive to staying in the crate than one with pent up energy. Walk him or her around the crate and let them smell and explore it. Be sure to have plenty of treats on you as you introduce them to the crate and reward them for good behavior. Eventually coax them inside with the treats. Leave the doors open so they do not feel trapped and can exit whenever they want. During play, throw toys in the crate so it becomes a natural part of their surroundings. It can also a good idea to feed your Golden in their crate. Keep positively reinforcing them and use praise when they go inside. Slowly your Golden will find it a place of comfort and will naturally go inside to rest.

Some dogs, usually older ones, will dislike going into the crate. There may be issues of separation anxiety or a mental block. Do not force or lock your Golden inside if it is showing signs of anxiety in relation to the crate as it will make the issues worse. We recommend seeing a professional and they will be able to help and diagnose the situation. In most situations however, if you follow the tips laid out above you should have no problems crate training your Golden.

Lastly, your Golden's crate is not where they are supposed to live their lives. So, do not leave them cooped up in there. They are part of your family and that is exactly where they long to be, with you!

Goldens are very smart. We recommend owners to stick to rules and training and not let puppy eyes get to them. Goldens can learn that certain behavior will make you do what **THEY** want. They can effectively flip the script and become the dominant one... this means they are training you!

THE WOOF BROTHERS

The Woof Brothers approved "Golden List"

It can be overwhelming for new Golden owners to make

sure they have everything for their new family member. We created a list of the common things every Golden Retriever owner can have to help out. Take a moment to review this list and see if you have everything you need for your new furry friend.

Golden List

🐾 Nutritious protein rich dog food.　☐

🐾 Water & food bowls　☐

🐾 A leash/harness　☐

🐾 ID Tag　☐

🐾 Collar　☐

🐾 Toys　☐

🐾 Blanket　☐

🐾 Bed　☐

🐾 Crate　☐

Golden List

- 🐾 Treats - for training & positive reinforcement ☐
- 🐾 Brushes ☐
- 🐾 Dog shampoo ☐
- 🐾 Toothpaste & Toothbrush ☐
- 🐾 Baby gates - incase an area needs to be sectioned off. ☐
- 🐾 Doggy poop bags ☐
- 🐾 Plan/organize socialization time ☐
- 🐾 Start basic training - enroll in a training program. ☐
- 🐾 Establish a schedule/routine ☐

Home is where your
Golden is...

FOUR

Speaking Golden Retriever

COMMUNICATION IS KEY

Dogs make all kinds of sounds from barks and howls to yelps and whimpers. Golden Retrievers are no exception to this. Just like how we talk when we have something to say, Goldens bark to express themselves. You don't have to worry about constant barking, however. Goldens are generally a quiet breed and bark occasionally.

Let's explore the main reasons Goldens bark. As you build a close relationship with your dog, you will learn more and more about what different sounds mean and their unique nonverbal communication.

Different Kinds of Barks or Sounds:

Excitement

Goldens love to play and can get very excited. They express this excitement by barking. Goldens can also be bored and want to let you know that they need stimulation. Take them out for a walk or grab their favorite toy so they can play. It will be easy to spot that a bark is out of excitement.

A Golden may also whimper and whine out of excitement. Whimpers can come out in several tones. Your dog can be excited about that afternoon snack you are about to give them and whimper in excitement. Normally they will be energetic, jumpy, playful, and lick you. A whine shows that your Golden wants attention, or desires something. It could be as simple as going out for a walk.

Distress

Any types of urgent distresses can make a Golden bark. Distressed barking can take a long time, and will usually continue until whatever the problem is, is resolved.

Reasons for this is:

- **Loneliness (separation anxiety):** If a Golden is left alone for too long, he or she will express it. They are signaling their need for attention.
- **Danger or caution:** A Golden is not typically a guard dog and rarely displays this behavior. However, if they feel uneasy about something they will signal it to their family/pack. There is a sense of urgency to this barking.

Goldens can also whimper and whine out of distress. This will normally be accompanied by the lowering of their heads signaling submission.

Lastly, if a Golden is in pain or shocked it will also

yelp. They use this method of communicating to let you know that they are hurting.

They make great watch dogs, but not-so-great security dogs. They'll bark loudly at strangers, but once they physically interact with a person, a Golden can't help but become friendly.

Fact Source: Kotch, R. (2019). *15 Things You Didn't Know About Golden Retrievers*. [online] Country Living. Available at: https://www.countryliving.com/life/kids-pets/news/a35634/15-things-you-didnt-know-about-golden-retrievers/.

Aggression

Goldens are a very peaceful breed. It is rare but they can show signs of aggression at times. This is only when they feel threatened. It is a signal to stop whatever you are doing with your dog. Assess what may be causing them to growl and leave the situation. Their growling is an instant sign of displeasure and aggression.

It is possible to confuse a happy play grumble with a growl. If you are ever unsure, look at your dog's body language. Are they calm and open or closed off and on edge? If you are still unsure, stop the game or activity and watch them. It is better to be safe than sorry.

. . .

Howling & Baying - Communication in packs

All dogs descended from wolves. A crucial way for these pack animals to communicate was through howling. So, some of these communication traits still have traces in the domesticated Golden. A Golden will howl or bay to alert you and your family... the pack! It is not common for Goldens to howl but a siren or certain high-pitched sounds may trigger him or her to start. Some Golden puppies practice it from a young age to alert their mothers of their location.

As you can see, there are a lot of different vocal methods of communication that your dog can use to let you know their responses to you and their environment. The more time you spend with your Golden, the more familiar you will become with these. Most of a Goldens communication however, is through body language.

Body language

Observing different facial features along with how they position their body, shows exactly what a Golden is thinking and feeling. Understanding this "body-language" will make the relationship between you and your dog much stronger. You will communicate on a better level and more effectively. As a general premises, dogs can do 3 things with their body which deliver different signals:

- They behave in a **comfortable** manner. This signals calmness and a relaxed state.
- Make themselves look as **big** as possible. This shows they want to be dominant and threatening.
- Make themselves look as **small** as possible. This shows they want to be submissive.

Goldens are most likely to portray themselves in a confident and comfortable manner. They can get very excited and playful but they will remain in this comfortable state. To further understand a Goldens body language we have to look at specific body parts including the eyes, mouth, ears, and tail.

Eyes

A Goldens eyes are usually oval shaped and relaxed. This normal state signifies everything from feeling happy, calm and relaxed. If a Golden looks at you and then away quickly it means they don't want to seem aggressive. On the contrary, if a Goldens gaze is fixated on something, it wants to get it. It may be a ball for fetch and this is great, but if it is on you, it can be confrontational.

Mouth

Besides barking, that cute naturally smiling mouth can also express a lot. When a Golden is panting, has their mouth closed, or slightly open it is a signal they are happy and relaxed. Yawning is a signal that they are releasing some tension. It is like a stretch and it shows a Golden is just trying to relax. An uncommon, but clear signal they are feeling aggressive is the showing of teeth and growling. This is rare but may happen.

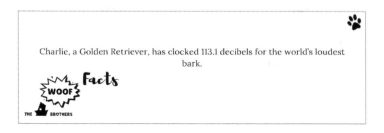

Charlie, a Golden Retriever, has clocked 113.1 decibels for the world's loudest bark.

Fact Source: The Happy Puppy Site. (2019). *Golden Retriever Facts - 40 Amazing Things You Never Knew - The Happy Puppy Site*. [online] Available at: https://thehappypuppysite.com/golden-retriever-facts/.

Ears

A Golden will also use those big fluffy ears to express itself. The more forward and high it positions its ears the more confident a Golden feels. If the ears are more flat and placed to the back, it is a sign that a Golden is nervous or fearful.

Tail

The tail is one of the more expressive body parts of a dog. A Golden is usually wagging its tail in a natural position and this is a sign for a happy dog. Some Goldens can get so excited that their tails wag so hard that their entire back bodies are also swinging from side to side. They are such a happy and excited breed!

When a Golden holds its tail naturally, level or lower than its body, it signifies that they are relaxed and calm. When they hold their tail tucked between their legs, it shows fear or nervousness. Lastly, if a Golden holds their tail up high and wags it slowly, it can be a sign of dominance. It may not mean aggression but one should be aware.

*Beware of dog...
it wants cuddles*

FIVE

Socializing

S ocializing a Golden is effectively opening up the first
door to communication with your dog. This is the first
step to better understanding your fur-ball. It is all about
getting your dog or puppy acclimatized to the sounds,
sights, and smells of the world around them. Socialization is
an important aspect of keeping your dog happy and creating
a safe atmosphere where they can be their lovable
selves. You are the leader and controller of the situation so
your Golden will look to you for guidance.

For all dogs entering a new environment socialization is
important, but especially for puppies. When a puppy is
between the ages of eight to twelve weeks old, there should
be a great focus on socialization. We recommend that socializing first takes place in a confined space or on a leash. This
way the owner can always stay in control of the situation.
Puppies or dogs should be able to explore the new area and
sniff around. For puppies this is a longer process as they
cannot take on all the new impressions at once. It would

make the little gal or guys senses overload. An adult dog will be able to explore the new area quickly and adjust to the new situation relatively fast. Puppies will need to start slow and then work their way up to longer periods of discovery and meeting new people and other dogs. Socialization needs to be in a controlled environment or on leash so that if something were to happen, you can take control of the situation quickly. This is especially true when introducing other dogs or pets.

There are two main risks owners should be wary of during socialization... injury and illness.

Injury

Goldens are all about playing... especially as puppies. While this is endearing to their family, it puts them at a distinct disadvantage when they meet other dogs. Not all other dogs are as playful, and because a Golden can have such high energy, it can cause friction. Certain situations can end with serious injury if the other dog is aggressive, or the Golden is still a puppy. If you socialize your puppy with other dogs, make sure you create a scenario where you can control what happens. Do not just put your Golden in a room with another dog and let them meet unsupervised. This can lead to dangerous situations. Overtime as it gains experience a Golden will learn how to interact with other dogs and animals. It will naturally pick up on the signals a new dog will give off.

. . .

Illness

Illnesses are common in young dogs. The best way to protect your Golden is to make sure that they are properly vaccinated. This way they can build up their immune system. We also recommend having a puppy only interact with other vaccinated dogs. Diseases can spread quickly from dog to dog, and as a puppy they are most vulnerable.

Socialization is a process that should consistently happen when a dog or puppy is in a new area. Puppies should start out with only a few minutes of socialization at first and then work their way up to longer periods of time. Socialization should be something that happens throughout a Goldens entire life. Explore new parks and areas, this will keep both you and your dogs minds stimulated.

*Everyone thinks they
have the best dog... and
none of them are wrong.*

SIX

Exercising

G oldens are a high energy sporting breed. Having so much energy means they need at least an hour of exercise every day. Without this exercise, Goldens can become bored and frustrated. This level of boredom can lead to destroying whole living rooms and digging up gardens. Goldens will find one way or another to release energy, stay active and not be bored.

Have no fear though! Exercising doesn't mean you have to go out and run for an hour every day. There are many ways to let out this high energy fur-ball. They are also great ways for owner and dog to bond.

Walking/Running

Walking is a great way to keep both yourself and your Golden active. If you enjoy going out for runs, your dog will enjoy accompanying you and the exercise. It is a great way to clear your head, and it is an activity where the whole family can be involved. Find a nearby park or just get out in the neighborhood.

Playing Fetch

Since Goldens were bred to assist hunters retrieve shot game, "fetch" is a perfect activity for them. Goldens will happily retrieve anything you throw for hours. A ball, toys, sticks... anything will do! It is a great workout for your Golden. Fetch can be played almost anywhere from the backyard to the park. On a day it is difficult to leave the house and an area in your home allows for it, a mini version can be played inside.

Hiking

Dog-friendly hiking trails can provide a nice change of

scenery for both you and your dog. Goldens will enjoy the combination of the physical challenge along with the mental challenge of discovering new terrains. Hiking is normally not suited for young puppies or older dogs. We recommend consulting a vet before doing very vigorous exercises with your Golden.

Remember to bring the appropriate gear and ample water for yourself and your Golden when hiking. This is also a great activity to do as a pack! Bring family or friends along to join in on the fun. Always stay safe and examine your Golden for ticks after the hike.

Swimming

Swimming is another great activity for your Golden. They love water and happily jump into any puddle, pool, or lake. They have water proof coats perfectly suited for being in the water. Swimming is also great for puppies. Just make sure to take it slow and to keep a close eye on them at all times.

Golden's are incredible swimmers. Their webbed paws and long tail that helps with steering makes them great water-based dogs.

Fact Source: Lessard, D. (2019). *10 Golden Retriever Facts You Need To Know*. HomeoAnimal.com. Available at: https://www.homeoanimal.com/blogs/blog-pet-health/81084420-10-golden-retriever-facts-you-need-to-know.

Training

Training can mean everything from agility training to learning commands. A Golden will love physical activities but will also enjoy any mental challenge. Explore what your dog enjoys as an activity and balance both the physical and mental aspects of training.

Games

There are an unlimited amount of games you can play with your Golden. We created a short list of game ideas you can play with your pooch below:

- **Tug of War:** Find a durable toy or stick and game on!
- **Frisbee:** Will be like fetch but it involves more challenging timing.
- **Hide & Seek:** You can hide snacks for your Golden to find, or you can hide and have your Golden find you.
- **Agility/Obstacle Course:** Guide your Golden through a series of challenges.

Life is GOLDEN!

SEVEN

Hungry Anyone?

ALL ABOUT THE DIET...

J ust like with humans, a dog's diet is essential to a long and healthy life. Not only does the Golden Retriever breed have unique dietary needs, each dog needs an individual meal plan. Activity level, weight, their coats, and age all play important roles in what they need to eat.

We recommend consulting your Goldens diet with your veterinarian. They will provide the correct advice for your Golden specifically. It may take some trial and error before perfecting a meal plan, however, this is perfectly normal. There is no one size fits all. What we can recommend for all dogs is excellent food quality. Many dog foods contain "filler ingredients" such as soy, rice, and corn. These filler ingredients do little in providing your dog with the important nutrients it needs. We suggest getting dog foods that have "high meat content". Some brands advertise high protein levels, but it is important to read the ingredients. It can be that the protein comes from vegetables and it is better for your Golden to consume actual meat.

Lots of Golden Retrievers are obese... Sadly, due to inappropriate diets many Goldies weigh more than they should, which can adversely affect their health. One study found more than half of the Golden Retrievers seen in a veterinary clinic were significantly overweight.

Fact Source: The Happy Puppy Site. (2019). *Golden Retriever Facts - 40 Amazing Things You Never Knew - The Happy Puppy Site*. Available at: https://thehappypuppysite.com/golden-retriever-facts/.

The Three Macronutrients

Protein, fat, and carbohydrates. Those are the three macronutrients, and a Golden needs items from each group to be healthy and happy. We want to stress again that it is very important to consult your veterinarian with your Goldens diet. A dog's digestive system is sensitive so you want to be safe with any changes you make and provide it with the correct nutrients.

The macronutrients a Golden needs can be calculated by their height, age, level of activity, and weight. We will dive deeper into some average estimates a Golden will need for each of the macronutrients below.

Protein:

An average Golden Retriever needs to have thirty percent of their calories come from protein. You do not want to feed your Golden less than this amount in protein as they are large dogs and they stay active. The protein will help your Golden maintain and develop their muscle mass.

Carbohydrates:

The amount of carbohydrates needed really depend on the activity level of your Golden and their age. Normally, good dog food will contain around thirty to forty percent carbs. If your Golden is particularly active, you will want food with more carbs in it.

Fat:

Fat content is essential in any diet, and for a Golden you want it to make up an average of fifteen percent of their caloric intake. Fat is good for them but it is not something that should be overly consumed. Goldens will happily continue eating past the point they are full, so it is a breed that can gain weight fast. Fat is essential in keeping a Golden's coat shiny and it reduces shedding.

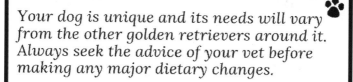

Your dog is unique and its needs will vary from the other golden retrievers around it. Always seek the advice of your vet before making any major dietary changes.

You do not want an obese or diabetic dog, so do not overfeed.

Treats

With those puppy eyes, their adorable behavior, and playful charisma it can be very hard to hold back from spoiling a Golden with treats. Difficult as it may be, treats should only be used as special rewards... not as daily snacks. Handing out too many treats can have a big impact on their diet. Goldens are a breed that can suffer from diabetes and overeating. As harmless as it may seem at first, giving out too many treats can create a lot of problems in the long run.

We are big advocates of using treats while training your Golden. Outside of training and reinforcing good behavior, we recommend keeping treats away from your Golden.

"

Always be yourself...
unless you can be a
Golden Retriever... Then
always be golden.

EIGHT

Health Care

The proper exercise and diet of a Golden lays a great foundation for its health, but more should be done to ensure a long happy and healthy life. Just like we need to go to the doctor for checkups so do Goldens. Regular checkups allow problems to be detected early so they can be treated. Below we will give tips and suggestions on how to find the perfect vet. This way you can make sure you have a healthy, energy-filled Golden for as long as possible.

Finding the Perfect Vet

You cannot find the perfect veterinarian without knowing what you are looking for. Each vet will offer you different services and options, and they might not fit all of your needs. Every dog and their owner will have their own set of priorities, and this is the best way to find a vet. You need to ask yourself "Can they satisfy my priorities?"

There is no harm or shame in shopping around for the

perfect vet. You want to establish you're Golden at a vet that will come to know them. This makes the overall care of your Golden a lot more consistent. So, start by writing out a list of priorities. If you are not sure where to start, think about the age of your Golden Retriever and any health concerns you may have. You will want your dog's care as specialized as possible. We suggest having a vet that specializes in dog care over a vet that specializes in a variety of different animals. This way you can feel assured that your vet is up to date on health concerns that can affect your Golden.

We summarized a list, of what we feel is important to look for in a great vet. Check it out below:

- **Ability to meet your needs as an owner.** Be critical about how they treat you, not just your dog. Did the staff seem knowledgeable? Did they answer all of your questions? Did you feel rushed or like just another number? You need to be comfortable and make sure they meet all your needs.
- **Their practice must be up to date and have some of the newer technology.** You do not want to see a vet who cannot stay current on animal medicine, as the field changes and updates regularly.
- **Do you prefer a smaller veterinary practice or a larger one?** This question comes down to preference. A small clinic will allow you to create a relationship with a certain vet, but a larger clinic can have greater resources at their disposal.
- **There is no shame in asking about pricing**, so ask away when you are trying to narrow down clinic choices. Also, consider how close the clinic is to

your home and their ability to make appointments around your schedule.

- They must be **knowledgeable about holistic treatments.**
- **Are they involved in their community?** This one might not be important to everyone, but it can be good to know how involved your vet gets with the safety of animals in their community.
- **Are they accredited?** Law does not require accreditation of veterinary hospitals, but it shows a certain quality. When a vet gets accredited, they present a promise to maintain the standards of care set by an organization. One of the biggest of these organizations is the AAHA (American Animal Hospital Association). They regulate the standards of patient care, surgery, and facilities that a vet offers. They also make sure that medical records are kept up to date, cleanliness, emergency services are offered, diagnostic imaging, and most importantly the continued education of the staff and doctors.

We also recommend asking friends and family for recommendations if they have pets. Word of mouth is still often one of the best ways to find out about great businesses! Some vets even give out discounts or bonuses for being referred. Either way, your friend or family member will probably share similar values with their pets as you would.

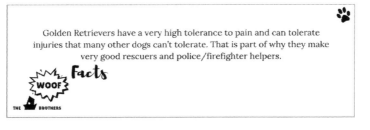

Golden Retrievers have a very high tolerance to pain and can tolerate injuries that many other dogs can't tolerate. That is part of why they make very good rescuers and police/firefighter helpers.

Fact Source: Lessard, D. (2019). *10 Golden Retriever Facts You Need To Know*. HomeoAnimal.com. Available at: https://www.homeoanimal.com/blogs/blog-pet-health/81084420-10-golden-retriever-facts-you-need-to-know.

Online research is also very helpful. Google and Yelp can help you find the top-rated vets in your area and also help you weed out the good guys from the bad guys.

The Visit

Once you have found a potential vet, we recommend visiting their facilities. It is usually possible to schedule a tour where you can meet the vet and ask any questions you may have. Here are some things we recommend you to keep in mind:

- *Is the vet's location easy to reach from your own home?*
- *Does the clinic look clean? Is the lobby organized? Do they clean up after every pet that's visited the exam room?*
- *Are dogs and cats intermingling, or do they have separate entrances and waiting areas?*
- *Does the waiting area seem calm and comfortable?*

- *Does the staff seem empathetic and are they happy? Do they stay calm in the face of pressure and bad news to patients?*

There are a lot of variables to consider when touring a vets clinic. We suggest trying to schedule the tour for a time when they say they are not too busy. This might give you an opportunity to talk to one of the vets on staff.

We also created a list of questions you can ask during a visit. Asking these questions can give you a better idea of how the practice is run and how the relationship with them could be.

- *What are your emergency care options? What type of emergency care does the clinic offer? If the clinic cannot provide you with emergency care, where will they then refer you to?*
- *Are they able to do in-house diagnostic tests? These include ultrasounds, bloodwork, x-rays, and other diagnostics. Are these tests referred to an off-site location?*
- *How do they monitor the pets that are there overnight?*
- *What are their payment methods? Do they allow payment plans or invoicing of clients? How do you make payments for big procedures like major surgeries or even consistent treatments for certain diagnoses?*
- *Are they involved with their community animal programs?*

Once you finished touring the clinic, you will have a greater sense of how it runs and if it will meet your needs. Tell the clinic what your priorities of care are and see how they respond. If their values and mission align with your priorities, then you will have found a good match.

Your vet should be perfectly happy to answer all of your questions. You are your Golden Retriever's advocate so it is necessary that your vet and their staff listen to what you have to say before determining what is going on with your dog. If you don't feel comfortable, look for a different vet. There will be one that meets your needs.

It's a two-way street

Once you have found a vet you are comfortable with, it is important to be as good of a client as possible to them. It is an important relationship that requires work from both sides.

Being a great client to your vet's office includes:

- **Arriving on time.** Try to arrive a bit earlier than your scheduled appointment time. This lets you fill out any paperwork, or complete any other small tasks.
- **Allow the vets to do their work.** The vet is the professional so you will need to trust them to provide the best care they see fit. It can be hard to let someone else take the lead, but remember that this is what they are trained to do. They know what to look for and how to meet your dog's needs.
- **Communicate effectively.** Ask for what you want

and what you need. Allow them to do their work but if there is something specific you would like, vocalize it.

- **Be patient.** Animals do not always act the way we want them to. If your vet is running slightly behind they were likely dealing with a difficult case. Waiting times can get irritating, but remind yourself they don't do it on purpose.

You and your vet should be actively working together to make sure that your dog leaves their office happy and healthy. So put your heads together, be respectful of one another, and you will be off to a great start.

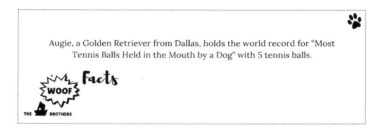

Augie, a Golden Retriever from Dallas, holds the world record for "Most Tennis Balls Held in the Mouth by a Dog" with 5 tennis balls.

Fact Source: Manzotti, R. (2019). *Top 10 Cool Facts About Golden Retrievers | Official Golden Retriever*. Official Golden Retriever. Available at: https://www.officialgoldenretriever.com/blog/dogs-world/top-10-cool-facts-about-golden-retrievers.

First Aid Kit

A first aid kit for a dog may sound a bit over the top for some, but we really recommend being prepared. For an active dog like Goldens we feel it is especially important. They sniff their way into all kinds of messes, so it is great to have things close by if an emergency happens.

It's fun to organize and put a first aid kit together. We suggest keeping all the first aid supplies in one container so they are easy to get to. (Keep it out of reach from small children and your dogs). Below, we created a checklist to help you put together a great kit in case there is an accident. Many items are common everyday things you already have in the house.

First Aid Checklist

Anytime you go on an outing with your Golden, make sure you have a first aid kit with the following items:

- Health history documents (Vaccine records, rabies documentation, etc.) ☐
- Your vet's phone number ☐
- A towel or blanket ☐
- A backup collar & leash ☐
- Bottled water ☐
- Extra food or snacks if it is a long trip ☐
- Collapsible food bowls ☐

First Aid Checklist

There are times when a slightly more extensive accident happens. When an abrasion or cut occurs owners will need to treat the wounds as soon as possible. This will prevent infection. The following items will help in those situations:

- Scissors & medical tape ☐
- Cotton balls ☐
- Tissues and wet wipes ☐
- A flashlight ☐
- Bandages & gauze pads ☐
- Tweezers ☐
- An antibiotic ointment ☐
- Disposable gloves ☐

Specialized First Aid Kit Checklist

Certain dogs have specialized needs. Perhaps they need to take certain medicines to combat allergies, or they are diet sensitive. In those cases owners will need to keep specialized items close by.

- Benadryl or other allergy medications
- Special solution for ear cleaning
- Antibiotic ointments
- Corn syrup for diabetes
- Pedialyte incase of dehydration
- Hydrogen peroxide & activated charcoal to make a Golden vomit. This may be necessary if they swallowed something poisonous.
- Nutritional treats & snacks

The face of a Golden Retriever feels like home...

NINE

Vaccines

Vaccines are extremely important to the health of your Golden Retriever. They work by strengthening the immune system of a dog so it can fight off different diseases. You want to ensure that they have an immunity to anything that might cause them harm. With new puppies adopted from shelters you rarely have to worry about vaccines. They are usually already vaccinated and ready to be brought home. We still recommend bringing new puppies to the vet to make sure they are in good health. Even if you have all the paperwork from the breeder saying they are fine, it is still best to get them checked up and established with your vet.

Not realizing the importance many owners let their dog's vaccines lapse and expose them to risk and danger. This can harm not only their own dogs but also the dogs they come into contact with. Staying up to date with different vaccinations will ensure that your Golden will remain as healthy as can be. We recommend discussing different vaccinations with your vet. The risk of certain diseases can increase depending on where you are located, so it is good to consult your vet.

The American Animal Hospital Association (AAHA) strongly recommends the main vaccines described below:

- **Rabies:** This is the most common vaccine and required by law. When a dog is infected with rabies, their brain will swell and they will behave aggressively. It is a highly contagious and fatal disease that can be passed onto humans. Rabies vaccinations come with a certificate for proof.
- **Canine Hepatitis/Adenovirus:** This vaccine protects a dog's liver and kidneys. A diagnosis of Canine Hepatitis means dealing with lifelong kidney problems and can be fatal.
- **Parvovirus:** This is an illness that attacks your dog's white blood cells. This is commonly seen in puppies who have not been vaccinated. The disease will cause your puppy's heart to give out. Parvo is highly infectious and can be easily passed from one dog to another.
- **Vanine Distemper:** This illness will attack a dog's spinal cord and brain. Once those systems are attacked a dog's entire system slowly starts shutting down. Vaccines are the only way to eliminate the spread of this illness.

Depending on your location there are more vaccinations that can be given to your Golden. Some areas in the world are more at risk than others.

When and how often do Goldens need their vaccines?

You do not want to get a Golden vaccinated all at once. This can overload their immune system. Most vaccinations have a schedule so dogs do not suffer too greatly from the side effects. They can risk different diseases if they are over-vaccinated.

Vaccines for puppies usually begin at ten weeks old as this is when the antibodies they receive from their mother's milk begin to die out. Rabies is the most important vaccine for a dog, and this shot is generally given at three months old and then yearly (or every three years depending on state/country) after that.

Your vet will recommend annual vaccines for different diseases. They will give personalized advice for your Goldens needs. The booster shots they recommend will help protect your dog against diseases and are important to keep up to date on. Do not let them lapse or you put your Golden Retriever at risk.

As with anything that is injected into our bodies, vaccines do come with their own set of side effects. Your Golden might experience some pain at the location of the injection. Occasionally you might see your Golden develop a rash, fever, or even vomit. In those cases you need to call your vet immediately, explain the symptoms, and follow their instructions.

The costs for vaccines will depend on your location and how many vaccines your dog receives. An estimated cost of around two hundred dollars annually should cover all of your Goldens vaccinations.

66

Golden Retrievers. Their
affection is timeless,
their devotion is ageless,
their love is forever...

TEN

Common Health Problems

Goldens are known for their beautiful coats, sunny dispositions, and playful buoyancy. Unfortunately, they also have some health issues owners should be aware of. Knowing these risks can help identify a health issue early and potentially save a life.

Joint - Health Problems:

Being that they are larger dogs, Goldens suffer from bigger dog health issues. Their joints face more pressure so it is important to keep an eye out for injuries in these areas.

Hip & Elbow Dysplasia

Hip and elbow dysplasia are one of the more common health issues Goldens face. It is a form of arthritis that is very painful and prevents a dog from moving comfortably. It occurs when there is an abnormal growth on the ball and socket joint of a Goldens hips or elbow. Normally, when a dogs hips and elbows are healthy, its joints fit perfectly into each other and allow for smooth movements. This allows Goldens to be the happy and active breed they are. With hip or elbow dysplasia the growth in the joint causes a disability and this makes it very difficult and painful for a Golden to move.

If you notice a Golden having trouble getting up or favoring a certain side, take them to a vet immediately. If hip or elbow dysplasia is caught early enough, some treatment or prevention work can be done so a dog's symptoms don't get worse.

Luxating Patella (Loose knees)

Luxating patella is a health issue where a dogs kneecap constantly moves out of its joint. This creates instabilities for the dog. Visible symptoms are limping, abnormal sitting, and falling. Just like with hip or elbow dysplasia it can cause a Golden a lot of pain. Visit your vet regularly so there is a chance for treatment and prevention.

SKIN/COAT - Health Problems

Those luscious, golden powdered coats Goldens have are beautiful and majestic but they do increase chances for some health issues. Ticks, fleas, or mites are difficult to spot in all of that hair and they can carry all kinds of diseases. We cannot stress enough the importance of maintaining a healthy coat for a Golden. Bacteria or mold can all make a Goldens undercoat their home.

These skin issues can also take place in the ears. Infections can take place there as well because they are so fluffy and floppy. Bacteria can easily get trapped in that area. If you notice a Golden constantly scratching or an odor coming from their coats, take them to a vet to get the area checked out. These coat type of infections are thankfully easy to treat, but the key is to find them early.

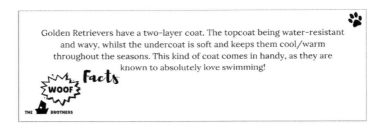

Golden Retrievers have a two-layer coat. The topcoat being water-resistant and wavy, whilst the undercoat is soft and keeps them cool/warm throughout the seasons. This kind of coat comes in handy, as they are known to absolutely love swimming!

Fact Source: PetairUK. (2019). *10 Great Facts About Golden Retrievers*. Available at: https://www.petairuk.com/news/10-facts-about-golden-retrievers.

Can you feel the heat? (Heat Exhaustion)

Summer brings with it hot temperatures that are sometimes too much for a Golden. With such a thick undercoat you need to make sure that your dog is not overheating. Even if a Golden is too hot, they will still be ready to play until they collapse. They cannot tell us verbally that they are over-heating so owners need to take preventative measures and keep a close eye on them.

A Golden's average body temperature is around 101 to 102 degrees Fahrenheit. They regulate this temperature through panting. By panting they expel any extra heat from their body. Sometimes in the summer months, they can not do this fast enough and this leads to a rise in body temperature. Even just a three-degree rise can have disastrous effects on a dog and their body.

During hot times we recommend always keeping cool fresh water around for your Golden. Please do not leave them unattended in a hot car as this can be very dangerous. Try to keep them inside as much as you can on a hot day. If they go outside, make sure it is an area with plenty of shade. Switch up your exercise routine to early mornings when it is still cool or do them later during the evenings.

Cancer

For humans and for dogs, cancer is a scary word. Unfortunately, Goldens have one of the highest cancer rates amongst all dog breeds. Much research is being done on why they have a high rate of suffering from the disease and how to best proceed with treatment.

Genetics play a large role in the likelihood of developing the disease. If two dog parents have cancer, there is a greater chance that their puppies will also have the disease. There are treatments and chemotherapy a dog can undergo depending on how progressive their cancer is. We encourage owners to take their dogs to the vet at least twice a year for a checkup. The earlier the disease is identified the higher the chance of treatment.

When everything in life fails... hug a Golden.

ELEVEN

Grooming Your Golden Retriever

BASIC CARE

Grooming a Golden is an important ritual. Their coats need to be kept clean and shiny. This not only keeps them looking their best it also keeps them in good health, away from ticks and fleas. Grooming a Golden is also a great bonding experience between owner and pet. Goldens love all social interaction and getting pampered is definitely not something they will run away from.

A Goldens coat will need regular grooming to maintain its beauty and function. They should be bathed monthly, and groomed weekly. There are times when a Golden may shed more and then it will be helpful to brush daily.

Some owners believe it is easier to keep a Golden more properly groomed and cool during summer months by shaving them. Please never do this. Their coats are perfectly formulated for their needs. They have a longer softer outer coat, and a shorter fuzzier undercoat which work together to insulate, cool, and protect the skin. Shaving their coats interrupts this process and will do a lot of damage. Their coats protect them from harsh sun-rays, keeps bacteria and parasites out, and helps repel water. A simple brushing routine is the only thing that a Golden's coat needs.

Here are some helpful tips for grooming a Golden:

Lucious Coats

Keeping their coats clean and healthy starts with getting a quality brush with good bristles on it. If a Golden sheds a lot, we suggest getting an extra brush specifically for their undercoat. Brushing a Golden with both their outer & undercoat in mind will greatly reduce shedding. A Golden should be thoroughly brushed once every one to two weeks. A Goldens coat grows quickly, and although shaving a Golden is a bad idea, trimming its hairs is not. Trimming their hairs will not only have a Golden looking neater it will also keep their paw pads free from tangled hair. They will have an easier time keeping their balance and keeping their grip as they run and play. Keeping a well-groomed dog will have them looking and feeling great! It will also have them shedding less and bringing in fewer debris from outside.

Mani/Pedi?

Besides a Goldens coat, their nails also need care. The main reason for trimming a Golden's nails is because if they are too long they can become uncomfortable, and even painful to walk on. Only clip or file the tips of the nails as they are sensitive and can bleed if cut too low. Clippers or files are available in most pet stores that sell dog items.

*Filing a Goldens nails can also help protect house floors from paw scratches.

Ear Care

A Goldens ears are very sensitive and should be cleaned/checked once a week. Besides brushing, Golden owners may also need to do some ear hair trimming. Some vets recommend owners to get special cleaning solution for the ears. Goldens are prone to getting ear infections, so please follow your vets instructions.

That Tail

Tails need attention and care. As soon as a Golden is awake it and its tail are usually in action. This means it is easy for it to get tangled and unkept. One of the best methods for grooming a Golden's tail is to gently twirl the end of the tail in one direction. Place a finger at the end of the tailbone and trim the hair there slightly. If a Goldens tail is matted, brush it out to make sure it does not get worse.

*It's not dog hair... It's
Golden Retriever glitter!*

TWELVE

Your Golden Retrievers Development

Goldens are born at a very early stage of development. Their senses are not yet fully developed and they need a lot of support before being able to face the world alone. For a newborn Golden every step is a mission. A balancing act that is easily distracted by new smells and sights. It is amazing to witness the growing process a Golden goes through from a small puppy to a senior canine.

Let's explore what a Goldens lifespan looks like in detail.

0-2 Months

New born Goldens generally have 7 siblings (littermates). From the second they are born they rely not only on their mother for survival but also on each other. They are blind, deaf, and have very little fur. Without their siblings there for cuddling and warmth they would risk hypothermia.

A Goldens first two weeks of life are all about survival and growth. Eating, sleeping, and growing is their only concern.

A mothers breastmilk contains everything a puppy will need.

After about 2 weeks of developing a puppy will open its eyes for the first time and their ears will start to function. A new world has opened up and their senses will remain very sensitive. A puppy's appetite will also grow and it will compete with its littermates for breastmilk. Curiosity slowly takes over as they figure out how to use their limbs better and can stumble around a bit more comfortably. Those vocal chords will also get put to use as they squeak and squeal out of excitement.

After 4 weeks a puppy is mobile and more alert to its surroundings. Socializing is a keyword for a puppy of around 4 weeks old. Now that it can see, hear, and move (relatively) well it will start wandering about, ready to explore. Throughout this first socializing period a puppies task evolve from only eating and sleeping to also playing. Playing is essential to its development as it stimulates the brain and establishes order in a pack. Puppies learn to follow orders and how to communicate with members of a pack. This is a very important time for development. Puppies that are not given the chance to learn these lessons with their littermates will develop poor social skills for the future.

As a puppy and its littermates continue to grow and gain strength, it becomes increasingly uncomfortable for a mother to continue feeding everyone. By around 5-6 weeks the weaning process will begin. This means puppies will get introduced to soft foods. It is a messy period as it is a new experience for the now very energetic and increasingly hungry pups.

By 7-8 weeks a puppy has learned a lot of its basic social skills from its mother and littermates. It understands its role in a pack and figures out that a human owner is the leader of a pack. Goldens are naturally a social and eager to please breed, so puppies will gravitate more to owners for attention. Therefore, we suggest adopting puppies at 8 weeks old. They have learned all the social basics from their mother and littermates and are ready to bond with a new owner. At this phase owners will also be able to start with some basic training. They will be open to new challenges and respond well to positive reinforcements.

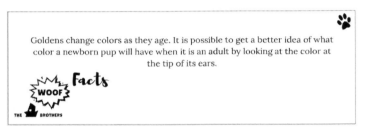

Goldens change colors as they age. It is possible to get a better idea of what color a newborn pup will have when it is an adult by looking at the color at the tip of its ears.

Fact Source: Lessard, D. (2019). *10 Golden Retriever Facts You Need To Know*. HomeoAnimal.com. Available at: https://www.homeoanimal.com/blogs/blog-pet-health/81084420-10-golden-retriever-facts-you-need-to-know.

3- 6 Months

At this stage of a puppy's life its energy increases daily and it is always playtime. It can be considered the prepubescent/pubescent age. Exercising and training is crucial at this stage. A young Golden will need to release its energy. Playing, long walks or runs are all great solutions. If possible, we also recommend joining puppy training classes. Not only will this help socialize a puppy it will also provide mental stimulation. Just like humans a juvenile Golden will look to test boundaries and show some nuisance behaviors. Anything chewable and gardens are at risk as they may chew or dig out of curiosity and pent up energy.

Some chewing can be cleared up as teething. Teething is very discomforting for a growing pup. We suggest getting some strong chewy toys for a Golden at this age. It can help the pain and will keep a puppy distracted from destroying other things in a house.

Put the chewy toy in the freezer. It will be more comforting to chew on something cold for a teething puppy.

We recommend stopping and discouraging any unwanted behaviors right away. It is an age where habits can form quickly and it will be difficult to make corrections at a later age. By firmly setting down rules & boundaries consistently a puppy will quickly learn right from wrong. Being too lenient and giving in to those puppy eyes will lead to big problems later in life.

Socializing is key and will set the tone for how their personality evolves. Although a puppy can get testy, it is important to make sure their environment is positive, productive and consistent. They may seem confident at this age but they are still sensitive. If they get frightened by something, it can have a lifelong impact.

6 Months to a Year

At 6 months old a Golden is almost an adult. Owners will look back and realize just how quickly time flew by. There is still a lot of growing and developing left to do for a Golden though. Depending on each unique dog it will either be relatively close to physical maturity or it will still have some growth spurts ahead. Often, their legs and tail grows first and fast. This can make them look a little funny until their torso catches up with the rest of their body. It may look a little comical but their growth can be irregular. By the time they are a year old their looks should even out.

Some Goldens do grow a tad too quick. This makes their bones and joints vulnerable. If a Golden is growing at a shocking rate, we recommend visiting a vet. They are at a higher risk for developing arthritis and other bone diseases. A vet will specify if a Goldens growth is healthy and regular or if some dietary changes should take place. Often, irregular growth is due to overfeeding and poor quality food. Proper diet and nutrition are incredibly important during a dog's entire life, but especially during their formative years.

Each dog is unique so the teenage or adolescent phase varies in length. Some Goldens will be fully mature by a year, and for some it will drag on. We recommend practicing patience and staying focused on exercise and training. Positive reinforcements work wonders and will ultimately help form a wonderful adult Golden.

A Year & Beyond

A Goldens life expectancy is between 10 to 12 years. They are very suitable pets throughout their entire life. After their first 2 months of life an owner will notice the breeds intelligence, and friendliness. They form an amazing bond with their owners and become a real family member. An owner will want to keep their beloved dog around forever. Below are some steps to keep a Golden as happy and healthy for as long as possible.

Exercise

Just like it's important for us to exercise and stay active it's the same for Goldens. It keeps them happy and at a healthy weight.

Good Nutrition

A clean and healthy diet is crucial in keeping a Goldens life as long as possible. Some dog foods have filler ingredients that do little in providing your dog with the important nutrients it needs. We recommend getting dog food with real ingredients and high meat content. Goldens also overeat easily. Too much food... even if healthy, is not good either.

Reduced Stress

Simply put, a happy dog is a healthier dog. Luckily Goldens are easy to keep happy. Enough play, training, cuddles, and good nutritious meals is all it takes.

Regular checkups

Regularly seeing a vet will help increase a dogs lifespan. Any diseases or problems can be identified early. This usually means something can still be done. Vets will also keep a dog up to date on vaccinations which will keep them protected.

66

Dogs come into our lives to teach us about love. They depart to teach us about loss. A new dog never replaces an old dog, it merely expands the heart.

THIRTEEN

Training Your Puppy or Dog

T raining a Golden is an important part of getting them ready for life with their owner or family. New dog owners sometimes struggle with the mindset they need to have to successfully train a dog. Goldens are used to living in a pack. In packs there is a pecking order, and it is crucial for both the owner and dog to see the owner as the alpha leader of the pack. This should not be confused with an owner not being allowed to be friendly and playful with a dog. An owner should just set and enforce boundaries.

Training a puppy differs greatly from training an adult Golden. Adults usually completed at least some training and know some basic commands. This foundation of commands makes it easier to expand on training. Goldens are eager to learn, so even trying to teach an "old dog" new tricks is definitely possible. Younger dogs and puppies however, start from zero. They still need to learn the basics and it can be a lot for both the dog and owner. They are still adjusting to the world so it is important to stay positive and consistent with them.

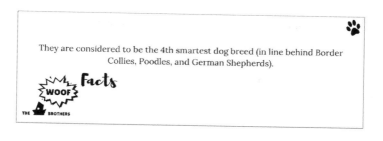

They are considered to be the 4th smartest dog breed (in line behind Border Collies, Poodles, and German Shepherds).

Fact Source: The Happy Puppy Site. (2019). *Golden Retriever Facts - 40 Amazing Things You Never Knew - The Happy Puppy Site.* Available at: https://thehappypuppysite.com/golden-retriever-facts/.

Learning the Basics

Young Goldens and puppies can be a handful. They are lovable fur-balls, but they take time, dedication and energy to train. Trying to put a leash or harness around a puppy can be frustrating when they lack simple training. They have so much energy and they interpret everything as play time.

One of the best lessons an owner can impart on a young Golden is attention and self-control. A young Golden is an easily distracted bundle of needs, desires, and sensations. A particular sound will grasp their attention for a second, and then an interesting smell takes over. Impulses rule their worlds... particularly at just a few months old. It's difficult to get some training in while they are in this state.

Self-Control Training

The most important thing to bring to a training session with a Golden is patience (bringing lots of treats doesn't hurt either). It will be hard to make progress without patience. This is especially true with puppies. They will not always get it right the first time and sometimes it takes trial and error to find out what works. It is usually a simple process that includes positive reinforcements.

Self-control will take plenty of repetition to instill in a young Golden. We explored some common areas where an owner can include some self-control training below.

Going for a Walk

When a Golden relates its leash with going out for a walk, taking it out can cause a lot of excitement. This overly excited state is not something we want to encourage. When an owner accepts this behavior and continues with the walk, they are rewarding the behavior. A better solution would be to put the leash down and walk away from the situation. Let the Golden calm down and then grab the leash again. Repeat this cycle, and every time the dog gets too excited put the leash down and walk away until it has relaxed and calmed down. The dog will learn that being calm gets them what they want - to get leashed and go outside.

Positively reinforce with treats. In the example above, when the dog is calm and sits, reward them with a treat. This will speed up the learning process and get a dog to understand what you want faster.

Leash pulling

New owners usually deal with a lot of leash pulling while going out for walks with their dogs. Goldens need to be taught to match their owners pace and follow their leader. It is great for a dog to have their freedom to explore but it is important that they can come back and follow the pace of their leader. There are situations, like when there is a lot of traffic where it is best for a dog to be on the side of their owner. Practice the steps below while going on a daily walk.

- **Don't forget the treats!** It is important to always have some goodies with you on a walk. It is a great idea to tie the bag of treats to your waistline. This scent will draw a Golden in and give him or her extra incentive to stay by your side.

- **Walk in a confident and relaxed state.** If an owner mirrors a dog's behavior and tries pulling and dragging him/her around, it will only escalate the situation. Instead remain calm and confident. Goldens can sense when their owners are tense and excited. We recommend staying positive and being very generous with treats at first. Reward your Golden Retriever for coming and staying close.
- **Have patience and continue to repeat the process.** Positively reinforce and reward them for good behavior. Over time a dog will simply stay by your side.
- **Cutting down on treats.** As this routine becomes a habit with a Golden, the owner can cut back on the number of treats. Rewards can then be given out more at random. It should take some practice and training before getting to this point.

Patience with Food

A great training tool involves a dog's food bowl. Practice self-control and patience by getting a Golden to sit before getting food. This exercise can be done with snacks alone at first if an entire food bowl is too big of a distraction. This way a Golden will already understand that an owner wants it to sit. Once the little guy or gal understands the drill of sitting and then getting rewarded we can move on to the same activity with its food bowl. Command the dog to sit before placing any food down for them. If the dog stands up or launches towards the food as it is being placed down, remove it and start over. Do not set the food down until the dog stays seated the entire time it takes to place it down.

Blessed is the person who has earned the love of a Golden Retriever...

FOURTEEN

Five Basic Commands

It is important for a Golden to know some basic commands. To stay safe outside, around other people and other animals, a dog should be friendly and controlled. Luckily Goldens can easily be trained and learn plenty of commands. All it takes is some consistency and positive reinforcements. We made a list of 5 basic commands to teach a Golden. They are easy to practice at home and on walks. We recommend joining local training classes for advanced training and the socializing aspect it promotes. These basic commands below are a perfect starting point for new owners.

Sit

This is an easy command for a puppy or young Golden to learn. Before feeding is a great time to practice this skill. The reward for sitting is the food! Have some snacks in hand and let your dog smell it. He or she will be eager to get the treats, so move your closed palm with snacks in it towards the dog's head. Keep moving it forward which will gently push the dog back and in a seated position. At the same time as the dog sits say "sit". If the dog is having trouble getting into position gently push down on its back area to get the point across. Practice this several times in a row and a Golden will understand the drill. Once the dog easily understands the command with treats, try the exercise with its food bowl. Goldens are easily influenced by food. It is a great motivator to use with training.

Down

The "down" command is another practical command for owner and dog. Goldens can be a quite large and excited breed which is intimidating to some. It's hard to imagine but some people get nervous around dogs... even adorable Goldens. Giving the "down" command can de-escalate situations effectively and put strangers at ease.

This is a great command to teach after "sit". An owner should start by getting their Golden to sit. Then, with a tasty treat in a closed hand, an owner should lure the dog downward into a lying position. It is import to say the command "down" as the dog lays down. Once the dog is down he or she can be rewarded with a treat. Keep practicing this command and soon a Golden will follow it without needing to be lured down.

Here

This command is interchangeable with 'come'. There are several other words or phrases that can be used - as long as an owner is consistent, a Golden will understand.

Training a Golden is a lot of fun with the right energy and if the correct techniques are used. For training the "here" command get a long cord that extends several feet. It can even go up to 30-40 feet. Attach one side of the cord to your Goldens collar and hold on to the other side as you walk away. Give a firm "here" command to get your dog to come. If it shows no signs of moving, then gently tug on the rope to move them in the right direction. Once your Golden comes reward them with a treat. Start with practicing the command from close by and slowly increase the distance over time. It is essential not to lose your temper or get angry. Continue practicing as much as is necessary with the cord.

Once the Golden comes without hesitation, we can begin

practicing without the cord. Don't forget... positive reinforcement is key.

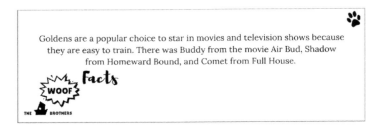

Goldens are a popular choice to star in movies and television shows because they are easy to train. There was Buddy from the movie Air Bud, Shadow from Homeward Bound, and Comet from Full House.

Fact Source: Manzotti, R. (2019). *Top 10 Cool Facts About Golden Retrievers | Official Golden Retriever*. Official Golden Retriever. Available at: https://www.officialgoldenretriever.com/blog/dogs-world/top-10-cool-facts-about-golden-retrievers.

Stay

The "stay" command is another useful skill to teach a Golden. It is one to easily combine with the "sit" and "here" commands. Once a Golden understands and has gotten grasp of the "sit" command an owner can easily get them to "stay". Once the dog is seated an owner can hold their hand up, palm facing their dog and give the command. The owner can slowly step back as their dog sits calmly and waits. In the beginning a dog won't have the patience to stay long. Reward all these shorter periods with treats and slowly increase the time the dog waits. With patience and positive reinforcements a Golden will easily get the hang of this command.

No

"No" is an important command for a dog to learn. With a puppy or a young Golden, new owners will probably use it a lot. It is natural for them to not understand all rules of a household yet or to test limits. It is a vital command to stop unwanted behavior. It is especially important for preventing a Golden from eating something they shouldn't, be it on walks or around the house.

Golden Retrievers do particularly well with modern positive reinforcement techniques, as they love spending time together and are very motivated by food and games.

Fact Source: The Happy Puppy Site. (2019). *Golden Retriever Facts - 40 Amazing Things You Never Knew - The Happy Puppy Site.* Available at: https://thehappypuppysite.com/golden-retriever-facts/.

This command is again easily taught with treats. An owner should hold a treat flat out in their hand, slightly less than a foot away from their dog's mouth. The dog will naturally go for the treat. When this happens, the owner should say the "no" command and close their hand into a fist before the dog can grab the snack. It is important for the owner to say the command with confidence and conviction. The owner should not yell but be direct. Often, Goldens will continue to grab at the treat. Be patient and usually after 30 seconds they will stop. Once the dog has calmed down, we can try the whole process again. Eventually a Golden will pick up on the command and understand the drill. Over time, an owner will be able to place the treat on the floor and practice the command. It may take some days of consistent training to get a Golden to this point. Patience and consistency is key.

Remember to have fun training! Enjoy the process.

Goldens are very intelligent and will pick up on these commands with relative ease. The consistent theme with these commands is positive reinforcement. To get the best results we recommend training often and in different locations. This way a Golden will feel comfortable doing the commands anywhere. An owner can also gradually increase what distractions are around. As a dog and its owner become more comfortable and confident, they can begin to use fewer treats. In the beginning treats are great to reinforce good behavior but over time a dog should perform the commands without them.

66

Nothing beats the welcome home from a Golden. The pure joy, the smiles, the wagging tail and the LOVE, LOVE, LOVE

FIFTEEN

Potty & House Training

Potty and house training is an involved process for dog owners. It's an owners responsibility to teach a Golden where it can go and it takes some time to develop this habit. Goldens aren't born knowing where they should and shouldn't go to relieve themselves so it can take months to train. Consistency and a controlled environment is very important throughout potty training. Instinctively Goldens don't like to relieve themselves where they live and sleep. A puppy or a newly adopted dog however, doesn't understand where it lives yet. Controlling their environment allows an owner to show a dog that the house is where it lives, and outside is where it can relieve itself.

It is important to frequently go outside with your dog so it has a chance to handle its business. After a Golden has finished it is great to positively reinforce the action by handing out a treat. This way he or she can slowly associate that this is where it should use the bathroom.

Follow the steps below to have more success house training a Golden.

The first 3 AKC obedience champs were Goldens. The American Kennel Club has been holding obedience tests for many years now, but the winner of the first three of these were all gorgeous Golden Retrievers.

Fact Source: The Happy Puppy Site. (2019). *Golden Retriever Facts - 40 Amazing Things You Never Knew - The Happy Puppy Site*. Available at: https://thehappypuppysite.com/golden-retriever-facts/.

Create a schedule and routine for your dog.

We recommend creating a food schedule. A puppy or young Golden will eat at least three good meals a day depending on their size and weight. We recommend having a puppy only eat within a certain time frame and then eating at this same time daily. This will get their bodies adjusted and in a consistent rhythm. Now an owner will better predict when a Golden will have to relieve itself.

This consistency can help prevent accidents and it allows a dog to build a habit for handling its business outside. It creates a learned behavior that is reinforced with encouragement.

. . .

Give praise when they go to the bathroom correctly.

Owners should constantly reinforce positive behavior. Goldens will not know they did something right unless they receive positive praise and interactions.

On frequent walks or trips outside we recommend owners to remain calm, and just let their dogs explore the areas without their interference. Only after their dog is finished relieving themselves, then give them praise and celebrate with them. Staying consistent with this shows a dog this is what you want from them. These rewards will lay the foundation for your dog's desire to go outside to handle their business. They will want their owners positive affections every time.

Never punish a dog for a potty accident.

Accidents will happen. It is important to never punish a dog for having a potty accident inside. It is completely ineffective and will only increase an owners and dogs stress level. If you witness an accident happening, quickly try to bring your dog outside or to a place where it is okay for him or her to relieve themselves. If it's too late, just clean the area thoroughly and move on.

---

*It is important to deeply clean the soiled area. Not only because of sanitary reasons but because of your Goldens strong nose. If they smell pee in an area they will instinctively try to pee there as well.

Pay attention to body language
Dogs will show cues that they have to go. Consider the following behaviors as signals that business needs to be handled:
- *Circling around a spot.*
- *Consistently walking to the door they go out through to go potty.*
- *pawing at this door.*
- *Sniffing an area strongly.*
- *Whining.*

A dog's body language can let an owner know that it's time for them to go to the bathroom.

Dogs will develop a preference for a texture to relieve themselves on. If they are potty trained to go on grass, they will eventually only go on grassy textures. Therefore, we recommend leaving the house frequently while potty training. It will prevent a dog from building a preference for relieving itself on carpets or house floors.

Owners often believe that their dog is fully potty trained too soon. It is not uncommon for potty training to take up to 6 months. We encourage owners to stay consistent and not stop the training prematurely.

If an owner is having a lot of problems house training, it can be best to visit a vet. There are many medical problems that can cause issues with toileting. If a Golden is having a lot of trouble, it can be worth going for a checkup, or meeting with a good trainer. They will be able to identify on a case-by-case basis if there is a deeper underlying issue that needs to be solved.

66

My sunshine doesn't come from the skies... It comes from the love in my Goldens eyes.

SIXTEEN

Eliminating Undesirable Behaviors

As adorable and fun-loving Goldens may be... they at times misbehave. Jumping, chewing, digging, and hyper-excitement are the more common behavior problems they have. Many new owners are lost when it comes to dealing with these issues. It is natural to want to fly off the handle and yell but owners should understand that punishment and yelling doesn't work. A dog will not understand what it's being punished for. Often, instead of stopping the misbehavior a dog will learn to hide the behavior from its owner.

The best way to stop misbehavior is through figuring out why a Golden is misbehaving in the first place. While dealing with many dogs and their owners, we noticed a trend. Owners who had one misbehaving dog would often come back with another misbehaved dog. Owners who had one well-behaved dog would often come back with another well-behaved dog. The problem rarely lies with the dogs but often with their owners. People repeat the same actions with their dogs which creates the same problems. All the solutions usually lie with the dog owners themselves.

Some of the most common issues owners complain about include:

- Inappropriate urination.
- Chewing on the wrong things and destroying furniture.
- Over excitement and jumping on guests.
- Strewing garbage around the house and creating a mess.

Below we will look into why Goldens misbehave and how to prevent it from happening.

Routine Makes All the Difference

Having a daily and weekly routine is an important step to raising a happy Golden. A routine gives the whole family/pack a sense of security and it ensures everyone's needs are met. Problems inevitably come up when there is no structure. Some activities that should happen daily in a Goldens life:

- Going for a walk and getting enough exercise.
- Eating nutritious meals.
- Socializing.
- Having some play time and training.
- Getting enough sleep and rest.

If these activities are not checked off daily, a Golden will probably act up. These are basic daily needs, so they will figure out a negative way to cope with unreleased energy, boredom, or hunger. These activities keep them mentally and physically stimulated. We recommend owners to keep a close eye on their Goldens and positively reinforce good behavior. Create the habit of giving the "no" command when they do something they shouldn't and reward them when they do something they should. Doing this consistently will allow a Golden to understand what an owner expects and wants from them.

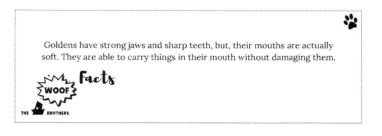

Goldens have strong jaws and sharp teeth, but, their mouths are actually soft. They are able to carry things in their mouth without damaging them.

Fact Source: Manzotti, R. (2019). *Top 10 Cool Facts About Golden Retrievers | Official Golden Retriever*. Official Golden Retriever. Available at: https://www.officialgoldenretriever.com/blog/dogs-world/top-10-cool-facts-about-golden-retrievers.

Isolation

Goldens are one of the most social dog breeds. They are family oriented and simply do not handle isolation well. Leaving a Golden by itself for too long makes it have anxiety, boredom, and depressive traits. If an owner needs to leave for a bit, we recommend exercising their Golden thoroughly first. This way he or she is more worn out and less likely to vent frustration and boredom by destroying a living room. It may also be good to have him or her rest in their crate for the time an owner is gone. This way they are less likely to hurt themselves and get into trouble. Their crate should be a spot where they can relax in and have a positive association with.

Unwanted urination may also happen if a Golden is left alone too long. Younger dogs will need to relieve themselves more often so an owner needs to be prepared. Especially when a Golden is in a new home or younger, we recommend owners not to leave their dogs unattended for over 4 hours. Busy owners should try to enlist the help of family or friends, or arrange a pet sitter.

Punishment & Corrections?

We briefly mentioned it above but punishing dogs when they misbehave is ineffective and can even have negative effects. We understand it is frustrating finding chewed up shoes or pillows, but a Golden will not understand why it is being punished. It is best to clean up the mess and create a solution to prevent the behavior from happening again. Severe punishment can cause a Golden to withdraw from their owner and hide certain natural behaviors around them. This creates an unhealthy relationship between dog and owner. Goldens should never be fearful of their owners and want to run away. An owners touch is something they should look forward to. As long as a Golden is trained properly with positive reinforcement there is no need for punishment.

How can owners correct any misbehavior then? We suggest owners spending plenty of time and supervising their Goldens. This way, when they act out an owner can correct the behavior immediately on site. It is important that the bad behavior is corrected immediately and in the best case during the act. This way a Golden will understand that this is not what an owner expects of it. If an owner is not consistent in correcting and sometimes allows the bad behavior, they are encouraging the act.

We recommend owners to interrupt the negative acts and redirect their attention to something else. Once a Goldens attention is on something else, it is best for the owner to positively reinforce the new activity. This means they should reward them with excitement, a treat, or some cuddling. Doing this repeatedly will prevent problems from growing or even arising. If a Golden is preoccupied with behaviors owners want from them, they will develop great habits.

At times, undesirable behavior can grow into a bigger problem. If it develops into something that an owner cannot handle by themselves a trainer or behavior specialist may need to investigate. All Goldens are unique and have their own personalities. Some may need a little more work than others. However, if a Golden has a good routine like the one mentioned earlier, and they are corrected properly, an owner will have a perfectly well-behaved dog.

Goldens are my favorite people...

_____

SEVENTEEN

Afterword & Summary

With the information in this book we hope we were able to show why Goldens are amongst the most beloved and popular dog breeds. These magical guys and gals become part of the family and teach us more than imaginable. We believe they are some of the best companion dogs out there. Our goal is to give Golden Retriever adopters as much information as possible and to make the relationship between owner and dog as harmonious as can be.

We covered a lot of information regarding Goldens, and it can be a lot to take in. In the following section we will summarize some big points as a refresher.

Golden Retrievers: Quick End Summary

Goldens are the perfect family dog. They are amazingly loyal, gentle, easygoing, and highly intelligent. These are all features that make them easy to train. Goldens were originally bred to help hunters retrieve shot game. They were a cross between a water spaniel and a yellow retriever. Although they are no longer only "hunting dogs" they still enjoy retrieving, so naturally love a game of fetch.

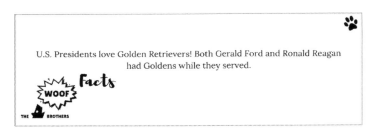

U.S. Presidents love Golden Retrievers! Both Gerald Ford and Ronald Reagan had Goldens while they served.

Fact Source: Petmoo. (2019). *Golden Retriever Puppies – Must Know Facts and Traits - Petmoo*. Available at: https://www.petmoo.com/dogs/golden-retriever-puppies/.

Family Adaptability & Help

Goldens are very social so they love being around their family. This combination of being a retriever and being social makes them the perfect dogs for active families. They are big time cuddlers, and even as adults they will not realize their size and believe they are lap dogs. It is common for a full-grown Golden to want to jump up on their owners laps on the couch to snuggle.

Goldens work well in all family situations. There are some breeds can only be kept if there is a lot of space available.

Goldens are simply happy when they are around their family. They can be kept in large homes with gardens, or they can adapt to apartments as long as they are let out enough for exercise.

The breed is very intelligent and they are happiest when they are challenged both physically and mentally. This makes them great family companions but they also excel as assistance or service dogs. Goldens are often used as guide dogs for the blind and for search & rescue jobs. They are eager to please and develop a great connection with humans. Goldens can sense how their owners are feeling. This puts them in a unique position and gives them the special ability to work with people who have PTSD, or children with autism. They have an amazingly calming effect on children who suffer from different stresses.

Physical Characteristics

Goldens are considered large dogs. On average, they grow to around 22 inches in height and weigh 65 pounds. They were bred to be working dogs so they have a powerful but mobile build.

The color variations on a Golden run anywhere from a reddish tone all the way to a light almost white blond color. The gold-ish yellow is the most common and recognizable coat color for a Golden.

Grooming a Goldens coat is an extensive process. They are double coated so it is a lot of work to get through all of that hair. The outer coat is longer and water resistant and the under coat provides insulation from colder weather. They shed a lot of hair, so daily or every other day brushing is recommended.

Training

Training and socializing is crucial with Goldens. They crave the physical and mental stimulation. In most family situations general obedience training is sufficient. One of the more important aspects with Goldens is recall or the "Here" command. Since they love being outside and playing, they can easily get distracted and chase something. It is essential for owners to remain in control of them and that they can recall their Goldens immediately whenever necessary.

Socialization is important with all dog breeds. Luckily Goldens love to meet people and see new places. The only issue owners can run into is over-excitement. They can get very jumpy and high energy when meeting new people. This increases the importance for owners to well train and socialize their Goldens.

A Goldens exercise needs are a combination of high and not so high. They are keen to spend time with their owners so whatever activities an owner is up they will look to join. They are happy with any activities... be it walks or runs, as long as it involves their owners.

Thank You

Thank you for reading this book and allowing us to share our knowledge of this fascinating breed with you.

For more information and to keep up with us follow our social medias and Youtube page.

Instagram & Facebook: @the.woof.brothers

Youtube: The Woof Brothers

If you enjoyed reading this book, please leave us a review! It will help us spread more of our content and create a better relationship between owners and their dogs!

Thank you.

Sincerly,

The Woof Brothers

References

Besides our own knowledge and experiences, we used the following sources to create this book:

Adams, John. "Socializing Your Golden Retriever." . *All About The Beagle Dog Breed*, 2011, www.dog-breeds-explained.com/socializing-your-golden-retriever.html.

AKC. "AKC Facts and Stats: Puppy Buying – American Kennel Club." *American Kennel Club*, American Kennel Club, 2018, www.akc.org/press-center/articles/puppy-buyer-fact-sheet/.

"Best Golden Retriever Training Guide." *Dog Training Excellence*, Dog Training Excellence, 2017, www.dog-training-excellence.com/golden-retriever-training.html.

Corona, Lauren. "New Puppy Checklist – Be Prepared Before Bringing Puppy Home." *Totally Goldens*, Totally Goldens, 2017, www.totallygoldens.com/new-puppy-checklist/.

Crazy Pet Guy. "Bringing a Golden Retriever Puppy Home

(and What NOT to Do) » Crazy Pet Guy." *Crazy Pet Guy*, Crazy Pet Guy, 9 Nov. 2018, crazypetguy.com/bringing-golden-retriever-puppy-home/.

Ducks. "Retrievers: Hunting from Boats and Blinds." *World Leader in Wetlands & Waterfowl Conservation*, World Leader in Wetlands & Waterfowl Conservation, www.ducks.org/hunting/retriever-training/six-essential-commands-for-retrieversbasi.

Geier, Elisabeth. "5 Steps to Finding the Perfect Vet." *The Dog People by Rover.com*, 31 May 2018, www.rover.com/blog/how-to-find-a-vet/.

Golden Retriever Club of America. "Selecting a Breeder." *Golden Retriever Club of America*, 2015, www.grca.org/find-a-golden/about-breeders/selecting-a-breeder/.

Knows, Scout. "Best Companions for Golden Retrievers." *ScoutKnows*, ScoutKnows, 5 Nov. 2018, www.scoutknows.com/lifestyle/best-companions-golden-retrievers/.

LabradorRetrieverGuid. "Be Ready For Emergencies: Essentials To Keep in Dog First Aid Kit." *LabradorRetrieverGuide.com*, LabradorRetrieverGuide.com, 4 July 2017, www.labradorretrieverguide.com/things-you-should-have-in-your-labradors-dog-first-aid-kit/.

Larson, Jessi. "Golden Retriever Price – Everything You Need To Know – My Dog's Name." *My Dog's Name*, My Dog's Name, 20 Nov. 2018, www.mydogsname.com/golden-retriever-price/.

Manzotti, Roberto. "Golden Retrievers and Food: All You Need to Know About Feeding Your Golden Retriever." *Offi-*

cial Golden Retriever, 13 June 2018, www.officialgoldenretriever.com/blog/health-nutrition/golden-retrievers-and-food-all-you-need-know-about-feeding-your-golden.

Manzotti, Roberto. "The Subtle Differences Between Male and Female Golden Retrievers That You Didn't Know About!" *Official Golden Retriever*, Official Golden Retriever, 7 July 2018, www.officialgoldenretriever.com/blog/management-training/differences-between-male-and-female-golden-retrievers.

Marla. "Male vs Female Golden Retriever." *Just For Your Dog*, 24 Feb. 2019, justforyourdog.com/male-vs-female-golden-retriever-which-one-is-better.

Meadows, Golden. "Benefits of Golden Retrievers as Family Pets for Kids - Golden Meadows." *Golden Meadows Retrievers*, Golden Meadows Retrievers, 13 Feb. 2019, www.goldenmeadowsretrievers.com/choosing-family-pet-benefits-golden-retrievers-children/.

Mircioiu, Andra. "Puppy Vaccinations 101: What You Need To Know To Make Informed Choices." *Totally Goldens*, 2017, www.totallygoldens.com/puppy-vaccinations-101/.

Pat. "What's Your Golden Talking About?" *Golden Retriever Rescue of Southern Maryland*, 21 Oct. 2013, goldenretrieverrescueofsouthernmaryland.org/2013/whats-your-golden-talking-about/.

PetCareRx., Team. "Golden Retriever Crate Training." *PetCareRx*, PetCareRx, 20 Sept. 2012, www.petcarerx.com/article/golden-retriever-crate-training/519.

Smart Dog Owners. "How Much Do Golden Retrievers

Cost?" *Smart Dog Owners*, 11 Aug. 2018, smartdogowners.-com/how-much-do-golden-retrievers-cost/.

Stevens, Kristen. "Golden Retriever Growth Sequence in the 1st Year." *PetHelpful*, PetHelpful, 2014, pethelpful.com/dogs/-Golden-Retriever-Growth-Sequence-in-the-1st-Year.

Wapiti Labs. "Common Ailments of Your Golden Retriever." *Wapiti Labs, Inc*, Wapiti Labs, 2018, www.wapitilabsinc.-com/common-ailments-golden-retriever.

Wendy. "Is A Golden Retriever The Right Dog For You?" *Totally Goldens*, 2017, www.totallygoldens.com/golden-retriever-right-dog/.

Wendy. "The History Of The Golden Retriever." *Totally Goldens*, Totally Goldens, 16 Feb. 2016, www.totallygoldens.-com/the-history-of-the-golden-retriever/.

Wendy. "What Is The Best Age To Bring A Golden Retriever Puppy Home." *Totally Goldens*, 2017, www.totallygoldens.-com/what-is-the-best-age-to-bring-a-golden-retriever-puppy-home/.

Wilson, Wendy. "Should You Adopt a Puppy or an Adult?" *Cesar's Way*, 22 May 2017, www.cesarsway.com/get-involved/bringing-new-dog-home/decisions-should-you-adopt.

Made in the USA
Lexington, KY
09 June 2019